There's a Part of Me...

JON SCHWARTZ & BILL BRENNAN

Dedication

The authors would like to dedicate this book to the Internal Family Systems community. Your healing impact is felt throughout the world.

Acknowledgments

The authors wish to acknowledge the courage, compassion, and clarity of the many contributors who shared their Parts stories and the power that this work has had in their lives. Furthermore, we'd like to acknowledge the following people for their contributions: Dr. Richard Schwartz, PhD; Toni Herbine-Blank; Dr. Frank Anderson, MD; Mary Mitrovich, Karon Brashares, Sandy Ellis, and all the CSL team; Kira Freed; Jose Nieto.

Contents

Foreword by Richard Schwartz, PhD ix

Introduction 1

CHAPTER 1   E Pluribus YOU 5

CHAPTER 2   The Inner Critic 9

CHAPTER 3   The Outer Critic: The Judgment of Others . . . 13

CHAPTER 4   Parts and Couples 19

CHAPTER 5   Parts and Bad Habits 25

CHAPTER 6   Protector Parts and Abuse 35

CHAPTER 7   Parts and Compassion 45

CHAPTER 8   Parts and the Workplace 49

CHAPTER 9   Parts and Illness 59

CHAPTER 10 Parts and Parenting 67

Conclusion 71

About IFS 73

About the Authors 75

Foreword

Thirty years ago, as a young psychotherapist, I stumbled onto the realization that my patients had what they called parts of them that could take over their personalities and make them feel, think, and act in ways that bothered them. Some of these patients were at the mercy of their binge eating, others were very depressed, and still others couldn't control their rage. I devoted my career to developing a way of helping those suffering with emotional problems to understand and relate to their parts differently and found that they improved dramatically. This journey birthed a widely used school of psychotherapy called the Internal Family Systems (IFS) Model.

In the process of finding this way of helping troubled patients, I and others began to notice that it wasn't just our patients who had inner parts—we had them, too—and that just being aware of and listening to them caused big improvements in our self-concepts and ability to live our lives more consciously and effectively. So what started as a model for psychotherapy has evolved into a simple, effective way to lead one's daily life with more qualities like calm, confidence, and compassion.

How is this possible? It turns out that simply thinking of ourselves as containing an inner community of personalities rather than just one mind is liberating and, as this book will explore, more accurate. For example, let's say that after fights with an intimate partner, you think to yourself, "I can't believe what a tantruming little child I can be sometimes" and vow to try to be more mature in the future. As a result, you walk around with a sense of yourself as basically an immature person who can sometimes act competently, and you beat yourself up in an effort to do better.

If, after an argument, you instead say to yourself, "I wonder why that young, angry part of me took over last night," you have a totally different view of yourself—perhaps as a healthy person who has an impulsive part. That's not all. Since you no longer consider it to be just a fleeting thought or emotion, you are motivated to form an ongoing relationship with this angry part of you. Then, when you sense the whoosh of its anger, you can quickly focus inside and reassure it that it doesn't have to take over and instead can trust you to handle the situation. You wind up with both a different self-concept and an increased ability to stay centered and handle your emotions. Your mysterious and uncontrollable moods start to make sense, and you have very concrete ways to soothe yourself and to better choose how to react to people and situations.

For many years, I have known that we needed a clear and easily understood way to describe this shift. Bill and Jon have answered this need with a highly accessible and well-written book filled with engaging true-life stories with which we can easily identify. This quick read can lead to a lifetime of more compassionate and conscious inner and outer relating. I am grateful to them for bringing it to you.

Richard Schwartz
October 2013

Introduction

There's a Part of Me ... is not about psychotherapy. It's about a way to use key ideas from IFS to improve your everyday life and your relationships with others. It's a way to understand yourself and learn to be a better friend, spouse, and parent—in short, a better person.

What do you think is your greatest personal struggle in life as far as your thoughts, feelings, and actions are concerned? Are you too angry? Sad? Do you gamble or eat too much? Do you strive for perfection but never feel you achieve it? Do you constantly judge other people and believe they judge you? Are you loved and praised by many, but deep inside feel you are not the person others believe you are? If you experience any of these or other struggles, you are not alone. Just being human means we will have problems in the way we think, feel, and act at some points in our lives.

This book is not about a new idea. It's about uncovering and using a powerful ability we already have to understand ourselves and what's behind the curtain of how we think, act, and feel. Once we apply this understanding to the problems in our lives, there is an instant shift in how we view ourselves and others, followed by positive changes in our thoughts, feelings, and actions. This shift begins to put an end to the negative patterns we thought would bother us for the rest of our lives.

Okay, we know — big talk. BIG, BIG talk. "Not even through the introduction, and these dudes are already selling the secret of self-understanding and solutions to problems. Whatever."

No problem. We get it. There's a skeptical part of you saying something like that right about now. We'll talk about skeptical parts later.

So, here are three simple yet powerful ideas we want to share with you that have helped people from all walks of life understand how humans think, act, and feel.

1. We are all made up of different "parts" that together form our basic nature and personality.

2. What we call "thinking" is often conversations among these different parts, each with its own point of view. Many of the emotions we feel come from these parts of ourselves.

3. All parts of us want what is best for us, and all of them contain valuable qualities and resources. But even though they want what's best for us, sometimes our parts have bad ideas about how to achieve this.

Normally, our parts work extremely well together. They coordinate, calculate, weigh in, and contribute to every decision we make, and they help us navigate a complex and sophisticated world. When they don't work together, we experience conflict. As we will examine in this book, ironically it is mainly the parts of ourselves that want to protect us from potential harm that tend to cause emotional upset in our lives. We will look at situations in which our parts are in conflict, learn how we can recognize when this happens, and understand what we can do about it. Through real-life stories from a wide variety of people, we will show you how a "parts approach" to inner criticism, insecurity, fear of judgment, struggling relationships, bad habits, abuse, problems at work, illness, parenting, and overall emotional turmoil can bring you understanding, acceptance, and happiness.

First, however, let's look at how everyone has different parts.

CHAPTER I

E Pluribus YOU

THAT'S RIGHT. To paraphrase our country's motto, "From many, you." Think of it this way. Most people are taught to believe that we all have one personality—one mind from which all our thoughts and emotions flow. However, going as far back as ancient philosophers, through the pioneering work of Carl Jung and other explorers of the psyche, to today's cutting-edge brain science, it has become increasingly accepted that our minds are made up of different subpersonalities, or "parts." Because most of us are constantly focused on our outer lives, we rarely see our inner emotional parts. When things are going well in our lives, our parts are in harmony, so they might not stand out enough to be noticed.

However, when things don't go so well or when we experience an emotion or thought that interferes with our life, we begin to notice that we have a number of different inner perspectives or feelings. Then we say we have ambivalence, or inner conflict, or that we are blocked, have out-of-control emotions or impulses, or intrusive thoughts. Usually, we don't pause long enough to listen carefully to these emotional impulses, intruders, or blockers. If we did, we'd find that they are not just thoughts, emotions, or impulses. Instead, they are parts of us that need our attention and compassion.

How many times have you heard someone say something like: "There's a part of me that really wants to have that piece of cake, but it will go straight to my hips" or "Part of me wants to go out tonight, but it will be too hard to get up early tomorrow morning"? While these are familiar thoughts, take a moment to consider what it would mean if instead of just being common phrases, these "parts" were actual, different aspects of our personality expressing their own interests and concerns? Sound weird? When you say, "A part of me feels that . . . ," you have already embraced this basic idea, whether or not you are aware of it.

Our different subpersonalities, or "parts," work together in different ways to make us who we are, all day, every day, in every situation and life event we encounter. Somehow most of us already know this—we know that we have different parts of our personality, some of which are at odds with other parts. Some of our parts are strong thoughts and emotions, some even extreme. Some are stuck in the past, when bad things happened to us or to those we love, and want to protect us from ever experiencing or feeling those emotions again. Others urge us to compete, control everything, or criticize or support our efforts and those of others. However, no matter how our parts influence us, whether seemingly negative or positive, *each of our parts wants what is best for us.* It just takes paying attention to what they are saying to understand and benefit from their perspective.

No matter how our parts influence us, whether seemingly negative or positive, each of our parts wants what is best for us.

CHAPTER 2

The Inner Critic

FOR EXAMPLE, THERE'S THE INNER CRITIC part of most of us, who always finds something wrong with our relationships, or our ability to manage our finances, or the quality of our work.

Larry F. is a 45-year-old college professor whose hobby is writing.

I'm a writer, and for a long time I had a problem. As soon as my pen hit the pad or my finger struck the first laptop key, I started to doubt my writing abilities. I would hear myself thinking: "Where did you ever get the idea you could be a writer?"

As hard as I tried to shake these thoughts, I couldn't. But over time, I began to see that some of my self-critical thoughts were valid. Since I never showed anyone my writing, who was I to say I was a writer? So I decided to embrace these thoughts and gave them a name — my Inner Critic. I began to realize that it was a good thing that my Inner Critic part was around, as he probably protected me from showing some really awful work to other people and really embarrassing myself.

Out of curiosity, I began to read books about writing that were written by famous authors. I learned that many of them had an Inner Critic, too, and that they had developed strategies, not to make their Inner Critic go away entirely, but to use it constructively. This allowed me to understand that my Inner Critic was just another part of me that protects me but needs my guidance and supervision.

Today I have a good relationship with my Inner Critic. I listen to his ideas and suggestions not as truths, but as his ideas, which I take under consideration. I share my work with others and find that, while my Inner Critic is right sometimes, often he is not. He's just overprotective and overly dramatic.

Notice the important change in perspective that takes Larry from "Where did you ever get the idea you could be a writer?" to "[My Inner Critic] is just another part of me that protects me but needs guidance and supervision." This is a main insight of the "parts approach." It is subtle yet very powerful. Larry came to understand that the "Where did you ever get the idea you could be a writer?" question should not be viewed as the whole truth about himself—it was just a part of his personality. He then paid attention to what his Inner Critic part was saying and learned to use its helpful perspective without listening to its more extreme criticisms. By listening to his Inner Critic instead of fighting with it, Larry learned that it was trying to protect him in order to keep him from being embarrassed by work that he had not fully thought through.

Larry's story illustrates an important aspect of the "parts approach": If you separate or de-identify from the voices of your parts, it opens up an entirely new way of relating to yourself and others.

If you separate from the voices of your parts, it opens up an entirely new way of relating to yourself and others.

CHAPTER 3

The Outer Critic:
The Judgment of Others

RECOGNIZING AND SEPARATING FROM PARTS of yourself, while acknowledging their concerns and getting them to trust your intentions, can be especially meaningful for those who have been driven to behave based on what they believe others think of them—by what others think they should or shouldn't do.

Consider the story of a daughter, Ann, and her mother's surgery.

I had always thought of myself as a good daughter. My mom means the world to me. She has always been there for me, no matter what. It's not surprising that when she told me she had to have major surgery, I was concerned and frightened that she would not survive.

The morning I took my mom to the hospital for her 5:30 a.m. pre-op check, I had only gotten three hours of sleep. I got a pager and went to sit with my mom until she went in for surgery. I can remember looking at her being wheeled away and wondering whether this would be the last time I saw her alive.

Two hours later, I received a page. I met with the surgeon, who told me everything was fine, that it would be several hours until I could see my mom, and that I should go get some lunch.

Feeling relieved, I left the hospital and went home. No sooner had I walked in my front door when the pre-op nurse called my cell phone and asked why I wasn't answering my pager. When I told her I had left the hospital and was waiting at home, she sounded shocked. "I see," she said. "Well, if anything important happens, I'm sure you'll make every effort to be here when you're needed." I didn't reply immediately, choosing to let her disapproval hang in the pause, then said: "You can be sure I will."

Thirty minutes later, I got a call from another nurse saying, "Your mom needs her teeth." So, I left home and delivered the teeth. I talked things over with my mom, and we decided that the best thing would be for me to go home and try to get some sleep since I was exhausted. As we said goodbye, the bedside nurse gave me a disapproving glance and said, "A little family companionship always helps." Finally, as I was leaving, I ran into the post-op nurse to let him know he could call me when she got a room. He said, "You mean you're leaving?" I looked at him and said yes.

I returned home and immediately fell asleep. At 6:15 p.m., a nurse called to say they were taking my mother to her room. I called my mother's cell phone, and she told me to stay home — that she was tired and would see me the next day.

As I was pondering the day's events, I began to realize how much I'd grown through my work with my parts. I was unfairly judged by three different nurses, and I had no reaction. In my "pre-IFS days," I would never have dreamed of leaving the hospital. I would have felt compelled to stay "just in case" I was needed. I used to be driven by fear of how others perceived me. In the past, other people's opinions or judgments of me would have triggered a huge guilt response. This did not happen. In fact, I took everything in stride and did what I needed to do to be a caring daughter and was also able to meet my own needs (for example, getting some sleep in a comfortable place). I did what my parts needed me to do to take care of them and my beloved mother. They trust me now, so they don't need to hijack me and control me. I was so pleased with the realization that my parts work is really paying off.

Ann was confronted with what she perceived as negative judgment from three health care professionals, and her perception was probably quite accurate. She reports that in earlier days, this judgment from others would have triggered her parts and "hijacked" her with feelings of inadequacy and guilt. As a result, she would have acted in accordance with what they thought was best in order to avoid incurring the wrath of the nurses and would have spent hours in the waiting room "just in case." Since listening to her parts and acting with integrity toward all of them, however, she's learned to do what's important for those who are most important and beloved in her life — herself and her mother.

Ann was able to calmly decide what to do without an onslaught from her parts. Through previous practice, her parts have learned that they can trust Ann to do what's best. As a result, she slept when she needed sleep and took her mother at her word that she need not be at the hospital to prove what a good daughter she was.

Parts relax when they learn that they can trust you to do what's best.

Chapter 4

Parts and Couples

HOLDING THE PARTS PERSPECTIVE is equally important within and between individuals who are in an intimate relationship. When you understand that you have different parts that can be loving and compassionate as well as defensive and aggressive—even toward your partner—you've taken a significant step toward developing and nurturing the intimacy we all desire in our relationships.

Sam and Teresa have been married for two years and have a new baby. Before they married, both had successful careers as freelance journalists, traveling to report on breaking news all over the world. Their lives were filled with spontaneity, thrills, and freedom.

When Teresa became pregnant, she was determined to keep working as long as possible and planned to return to work after seven weeks. But things didn't work out that way. When the baby came home, the young couple faced what every young couple faces — the overwhelming sense of responsibility for this tiny, helpless creature they had brought into the world. When the seven-week mark came and went, and it was time to place the baby in infant day care, it was obvious to both of them that despite their plans, they couldn't leave their baby with strangers.

Sam got a staff job at a magazine. It wasn't what he wanted, but the job had health benefits. Teresa stayed home and took care of the baby and kept house.

Sam had to travel a good deal, often worked late, and usually came home tired. Teresa was alone most days, felt isolated, and missed her old job. This arrangement began to take its toll on their relationship, and soon they began to fight over little things. Teresa told Sam he needed to help with the housework, and Sam said she had all day to do it while he had to work. There were arguments over who needed to spend time with the baby as well as what to do when they got a sitter and had the chance to go out.

One Friday, Sam came home late from work on a night they had planned to go out. Teresa was furious.

"You know, I'm starting to think that this isn't working," she said. You can't even get home the one night we planned on."

Sam threw his briefcase on the table. "Yeah — well, if you had to take the shit I take every day at my shit job, you would understand."

"Well, I don't. And you don't understand what my life is like, and you don't seem to care, either."

"I don't care? That's what you're saying to me? I understand all right. You're an ungrateful, spoiled bitch who only thinks about what's wrong with me and our life."

"I hate you right now."

"Good, that will make it easier. I want out."

Stunned, Teresa burst into tears, ran into their bedroom, and slammed the door. As Sam considered what he'd just said, he felt the energy drain from his body. He dropped to the couch, his heart racing.

Sam and Teresa triggered parts in each other that took over and hijacked them both, which led to this exchange between them. This is a common process among couples, and it has the potential to damage and sometimes ruin relationships. However, there is a way to avoid these kinds of exchanges. The key is to be able to hold the parts perspective about yourself and your partner. This is done by the simple (but not easy) act of speaking *for* rather than *from* your parts.

If Teresa had said, "A part of me hates you right now," Sam would have gotten an entirely different message than when she said, "I hate you right now." This is partly because the former words remind Sam that it is just a part of her, not all of her. It is also because when you speak for a part, you have to separate from it to some degree, so what you say doesn't carry the same level of emotional charge or contempt as when the part totally hijacks you and you only speak from its perspective.

The "parts approach" gives you the space to consider different responses to emotional triggers from other people or events. For Sam and Teresa, if Sam says, "A part of me wants out," it frees up the idea that the rest of him still values the relationship. If he says it to himself, internally, it makes it clear that there are multiple feelings at play. If he says it out loud to Teresa, her reaction is likely to be a lot softer because she understands that only a part of him, not all of him, feels that way.

Consider how differently things might have worked out for Jason and his wife if they'd had this ability.

> IFS has given me a lot. One of the simplest pieces is helping me relate to my ex-wife.
>
> I can remember moments in our marriage when she would be very loving toward me — telling me how much she appreciated me being her husband. And what seemed like moments later, she would open an envelope from the bank and learn I'd overdrawn our checking account by $5 and been charged a $25 bank fee, and she'd be furious toward me. Back then, I was shocked and horrified. I had no map in my head to unite these two completely different people. I could only think that the furious part was the "real" her, and the part that told me she loved me was "fake" because it would go away if she got upset. That was a deeply troubling story to believe.
>
> Now, looking back, it seems so simple and clear that she must have a part that is deeply worried about finances, and

when she read the letter, it triggered that deep anxiety, and a protective part leapt to her rescue and turned the attack away from her and toward me. Thanks to my new understanding, I can find peace. There was nothing wrong with me or her, only that we didn't know how to locate and listen to our own parts or each other's parts. We didn't even know we had parts at all.

Had Jason's wife known how to speak for her parts rather than from them, and had Jason been able to understand that his wife was speaking from a protective part, not her whole self, perhaps their marriage could have survived. The new understanding Jason refers to is the IFS "parts approach," which is potent and liberating for relationships and available to everyone.

Chapter 5

Parts and Bad Habits

A COMMON PROBLEM THAT MANY PEOPLE FACE is compulsive behavior, which can take the form of bad habits and, in the worst cases, addiction. These self-defeating behaviors are an excellent place to learn about your parts. If, instead of ignoring the problem, we paused and looked inward, we would find that many of these thoughts and impulses are parts of ourselves that need our attention and compassion.

We may find ourselves in the "habit" of smoking, drinking, overeating, being unfaithful, or working too much. But if we can learn what our parts want for us, what they believe we need, and why they encourage and nourish thoughts, feelings, and actions that make up their part of the habit, we can effectively and mindfully help our parts change course. Like all things, practice makes perfect. It took practice to establish the habit, and it will take practice to break it. We can move away from those things that trouble and disturb our lives. We can break the habit. We can change.

Jack put on about twelve pounds this past year as a result of an eating cycle that probably started in college, when late-night hunger gave way to pizza orders, funds permitting.

His eating cycle goes something like this: He doesn't eat much in the morning, has a big lunch, and finishes a full dinner by 6:30 p.m. Even though he's eaten until he's full, he somehow finds his way to an additional caloric binge sometime between 7:30 and 11:00 p.m.

A Compulsive Part of him then says, "Ice cream would be good right now" as he gets up with belly distended from a big dinner.

Jack goes to bed, but before he falls asleep, his Shame Part says, "How could you let that happen again?" But he falls asleep within seconds, as he always does.

After a couple hours of sleep, Jack leaps out of bed because he's gagging on a little bit of his own vomit. It appears that the bingeing has reached a critical mass, and before he's even fully awake, he's gasping for air in the bathroom and rinsing out his mouth. Jack goes back to bed but not back to sleep. He knows he'll be up for a while. His Shame Part is now in full control. All he can think about is how stupid, demeaning, and unnecessary the whole thing is. After minutes give way to an hour or more, Jack's Shame is met by his Hope Part — hope that tomorrow and hereafter will be different. It must be different. His Hope Part says that there's nothing at all stopping him from ending such eating behavior and no reason at all not to change. His Hope Part can see the future Jack—a future of sensible eating and peaceful sleep with no more tempting Compulsive or guilt-inflicting Shame parts.

Jack wakes up the next day, and yet another part of him laughs with contempt at his stupidity and his shame and hope. This is the "Dealing with Real Life" Part of Jack. This part would never have anything to do with the Shame Part, the Hope Part, or the Compulsive Part that led him to binge in the first place. He has no time for all this drama and insanity. This inner chatter is not for him. He needs to get on with things and take care of business. He's dealing with real life here.

How did Jack get here? What caused this cycle and Jack's inability to break free of it? And what's the deal with these parts of Jack that come to life and take over at precisely the same moments within this cycle?

These are questions all of us have asked ourselves in the face of habitual behavior. But what can we do to better understand what's going on? It turns out that if we can learn to "listen" to the "voice" that is asking those questions, we realize that the voice is coming from a part of us—a part that is frustrated by our failure, over and over again, to break the cycle. If we take this one step further and actually talk with all the different parts of ourselves that keep us locked in unhealthy habits, we can learn how to free ourselves.

Let's stop here and acknowledge an important point. Talking to parts of ourselves sounds weird, and it's common for people to be skeptical. Most people are until they learn, through practice, how to do this. It's one of those things that may be difficult to accept until you've experienced it. Until you focus inside, begin intentional conversations with your thoughts and emotions, and listen to the answers that come, this will be very hard to believe. But you needn't take this on faith. If you keep your mind open to this possibility and do your own exploring, you'll find out for yourself—that you can help your inner weaknesses or problem parts become your allies.

So what can Jack do? Jack decides to use the IFS method of speaking directly to the different parts of himself that keep him locked in this habit.

JACK (to Compulsive Part): Would it be okay if I asked you a few questions?

COMPULSIVE PART: Sure.

JACK: Okay, thanks. What is it you want for me?

COMPULSIVE PART: Just to enjoy life.

JACK: By eating ice cream?

COMPULSIVE PART: Sure.

JACK: What more do you want for me?

COMPULSIVE PART: You need to do less. You need to have fun. You need to stop making every day a race to get stuff done. You need to feel *good!*

JACK: And ice cream makes me feel good?

COMPULSIVE PART: Yes.

Jack hears that this Compulsive Part wants him to feel good.

Compare this dialogue with the Shame Part dialogue, which goes something like this:

JACK: What is it you want for me?

SHAME: I want you to stop acting crazy. I want you to stop doing a crazy thing just before bed that you know is stupid and makes you feel awful and lose sleep.

JACK: You feel that eating ice cream just before bed after a full dinner is crazy?

SHAME: Yes, and you *know* it's crazy!

JACK: What more do you want for me?

SHAME: I want so badly for you to break this crazy cycle you're on. I want you to go to bed without being stuffed with crap. I want you to feel good.

So, it turned out that Jack's Compulsive Part and the Shame Part have the same goal: They both want him to feel good. They both think that's what's best for him, yet they are causing conflict within Jack.

Jack has similar conversations with his Hope Part and his "Dealing with Real Life" Part, with the same results. Each part wants what's best for him and thinks it knows how to get it.

Where previously Jack was disgusted with himself for the late-night ice cream binge and with the Compulsive Part that led the way, this inner exercise has given him an understanding of why this happens, and he has developed an understanding of his parts that are involved in this cycle.

With this knowledge, Jack goes back and negotiates with his Compulsive Part:

JACK: Thank you for wanting what's best for me. I appreciate you looking out for me so I can have more joy in my life. What if we looked at a different way to find joy? The ice cream binge causes a whole lot of problems for me.

COMPULSIVE PART: What do you have in mind?

JACK: I'd like to play with the dog before bedtime. That's fun for me. Eating ice cream feels good, but then later it feels really bad.

COMPULSIVE PART: I'm willing to give it a try.

Jack then has a similar conversation with the other parts in this eating cycle:

JACK (to Shame Part): It's clear to me that you want what's best for me, and I'm grateful that you want to help me. I'd like it if you wouldn't overwhelm me in the middle of the night with guilt and self-hate when there's nothing I can do about it right then. I'd like you to be able to relax more so I can sleep better and let me deal with my problem when it won't cause me another one—no sleep.

SHAME PART: I'll do my best.

JACK (to Hope Part): It's clear to me that you want what's best for me, and I'm grateful that you want to help me. I'd like you to be patient with me and where I'm trying to go with my life. I'd like you to not overwhelm me with big, optimistic plans for changes in the future and trust that things will work out. I'd like you to be able to relax and not spin tales in the middle of the night.

HOPE PART: Okay.

JACK (to Dealing with Real Life Part): It's clear to me that you want what's best for me, and I'm grateful that you want to help me. I appreciate your real-world approach to life and how good you are at taking care of business, but I'd like you to find it in your heart to be more compassionate and less angry toward my other parts. They also want what's best for me.

DEALING WITH REAL LIFE PART: Okay.

This view of our inner world—of parts and the place from which we can help lead our parts (known in IFS as "the Self")—provides a way to change our patterns or cycles. If we act differently, it affects the way we think and feel about ourselves.

> *You can help your inner weaknesses or problem parts become your allies.*

All intentional changes in our lives, including learning to end habits that we find harmful—whether learning to stop eating ice cream late at night, quitting smoking or drinking or drugs, or even taming a bad temper—require hard work and practice. It is not realistic to expect to have one of these "inner dialogues" and, miraculously, all is well and all the choices you make become good ones. However, the self-acceptance that comes with understanding not only about your parts' existence but also their value and their benevolence toward you provides a greater inner compassion. In turn, this creates an inner environment in which the changes you seek become easier to attain.

There is an old story about the wind and the sun. Wind and Sun were hanging out one day when they saw a man walk by with a coat on. Wind offered a bet with Sun that he could get the man to take his coat off more successfully than Sun could. Sun accepted the wager.

Wind proceeded to blow hard at the man. The man clutched his coat. Wind blew harder and colder, and the man held his coat tighter. The harder Wind blew, the tighter the man held to his coat, even when the wind was blowing the man right off his feet!

Sun said, "Let me try" and proceeded to shine its warmth on the man. The man loosened his coat and slowed his walking. Sun shined warmer, and the man lay down on the grass and took off his coat.

Our parts are like the man. If we approach our parts as the sun did, they will feel the warmth of our understanding, and they'll relax and become more willing to change what they do. As they change, we change.

> *The "parts approach" creates an inner environment in which the changes you seek become easier to attain.*

CHAPTER 6

Protector Parts and Abuse

THE FOLLOWING STORY IS ABOUT HOW OUR PARTS are fundamental elements of our nature, of our being, and how they are working all the time just outside our consciousness. It is also a story of how our parts can adapt to very trying, traumatic experiences and "take control" to cope with desperate circumstances and lead us out in the best way they know.

My name is Michael. When I was about eight years old, one of the older boys in my neighborhood, Jeremy, asked if I'd like to spend the night at his house along with another older boy, Del. I remember feeling a bit iffy about his invitation because Jeremy and other kids in my neighborhood had been cruel to me in the past. But this made me anxious for things to be better, and staying the night at Jeremy's was the hopeful thing to do, so it felt like the right thing to do.

It wasn't.

At first the night was fun, and I was happy that I'd been invited. As the night wore on, however, Jeremy said that it was time to start "practicing for girls." He and Del started making out with each other and then with me in a very sudden fashion. I remember having this strange out-of-body feeling that I was one of three boys kissing and grabbing each other, and then it hit me that this wasn't right. I told Jeremy and Del that I thought this was wrong, that we should stop. Jeremy explained that "it didn't make me a fag" and that it was just practice for girls, so it was okay to do it.

I remember waking up in the dead of night with the profoundest feeling of shame — stronger than any I've ever felt in my life, before or since. "How could you have done this?" I heard my Shame Part exclaim. "You are a dirty, gross pig, you're a . . ." The shame was so overwhelming that I wanted to escape from my own skin.

After some time, my Shame Part gave way to my Hope Part. I remember that a glorious feeling came over me, that perhaps there was a way out of this horrible thing I had done. My Hope Part had a plan: I would wake up tomorrow and go home and tell my mom and dad everything, and they'd forgive me. They'd make sure I never had to spend the night at Jeremy's again, and they'd keep my secret, and I would pull through all of this. No one else would know, not even my brothers, which meant that no one would hate me.

I finally fell back to sleep. The second I woke up, my poor Hope Part, which had worked so hard and come up with a really good plan, was confronted by my "Deal with Reality" Inner Critic Part, which crushingly announced that no way was I going to run home and tell Mom and Dad. It'd never work. My Inner Critic Part obliterated this plan, and I once more felt profoundly sick and disgusted with myself and with these two boys, whom I couldn't tolerate being around.

I told Jeremy that I needed to go without staying for breakfast. He eyed me closely as I left.

"Remember, it was just practice. And it's our secret. Don't say anything. Alright, Mikey?"

"Alright."

"Because if you say anything, you know what'll happen?"

"What?"

"Everyone will know you're a little faggot, and I'll beat your ass."

"Okay, I won't say anything."

"Really. I'll kill you if you do."

I went home and went to my room. I never said a word about any of what happened to my parents or anyone else for a very long time. Today, I believe that this was an important decision. I believe that had I followed the plan developed by my Hope Part, I may have been a very different person because my parents were very good people who loved their children. But it was not to be because my "Deal with Reality" Inner Critic Part was in charge. This part of me saw "reality" in a very skewed way — that I had done something gross and disgusting, and this bad thing happened because I was bad. It never occurred to this part that it was okay to tell my parents, that they'd help. It had decided that a full confession to my parents was too risky. Others would surely find out.

Unfortunately, Jeremy, Del, and a few other boys in the neighborhood weren't done. The last time was the worst. Jeremy and Del were joined by two other boys who were two and three years older than me. I was held down by three of them while Jeremy forced himself on me. It was really bad. I was taken over by a part of me that I believe, looking back, is universal to all people who are physically, sexually, or emotionally abused, coerced, and manipulated. It's a part that says, "We can get through this; just get through this and we'll be done. It'll be okay. It'll be over soon." This part accepted that I was trapped and that I would have to learn to live with this terrible situation. This part protected me, got me through, told me I'd be okay. It was my Protector Part. To this very day, I'm grateful for this part stepping up to care for me during such a horrible series of situations and the work it had to do.

Weeks later, Jeremy and two other kids cornered me again and said they want to go back to Jeremy's room. I said no. The word just popped out of my mouth without any thought.

"No."

"You'd better start walking to my house — now, Mikey."

"No." I started walking in the direction of my house.

"You'd better start walking to my house now, or I will fucking kill you!"

"I don't care. I'm not going." I walked on.

They smacked me a few times on the back of the head,

but it didn't hurt. I was protected. My Protector Part was seeing that, in fact, I was making my way home, and they couldn't stop me. This was all I knew. I had to make it home.

Happily, nothing ever happened again. Jeremy tried a couple more times to scare me into coming to his house, but each time, with greater strength, conviction, and confidence, I said no. My worst fears were never realized.

Children's assumptions about events are often wrong and made from a lack of understanding. For me, the risk of being exposed, coupled with the conviction that the bad thing happened because I was bad, compelled my Protector Part to strategize how to live with this secretly rather than go outside the situation and look for help. This part is universally recognizable to abuse victims who have a perceived mandate that the abuse be kept hidden from others.

After the "Jeremy years," I changed. I developed an unhealthy and exaggerated hatred of my brothers and my parents through most of my teen years. I also gravitated toward things that would make me feel tough—football, boxing, rugby. I got into an inordinate number of fistfights and developed a penchant for shoplifting immediately after the "Jeremy years." I wasn't myself. I had been a boy who came by smiling, laughing, and compassion very easily, but these tendencies had been greatly blunted.

During this period, my Protector Part did one more enormous thing: It shut down the running, internal monologue I had about the "Jeremy years." And then I stopped remembering them altogether. I repressed the memory of that time — all of it. My Protector Part recognized that the memory was too painful and that it was better to lock the memory away than to be aware of it. I suspect that had I maintained an awareness of these events, I probably would have been incapacitated by the shame I felt for what I'd done. At that young age, I still saw all of it as "what I'd done," not "what they'd done." This makes all the difference. My Protector Part took away these memories, and I got on with my life, albeit a changed life.

. . .

When I was twenty-four years old, I dated a woman, Kerri, who was very nice, and we enjoyed each other's company. After several months of dating, I found it increasingly curious that she never wanted to spend time at her home. She often spoke of how she preferred to avoid being there when her roommate was around. Then one day she said she had something to tell me.

Through torrents of tears, she confessed that her desire to avoid meeting at her house was because her roommate was, in fact, her lesbian partner. She spoke of the profound shame she felt for how she'd kept this not only from me but also kept her relationship with me from her partner. Her sense of shame was multilayered, as she hadn't disclosed her sexual orientation issues to her own family and close friends.

I wasn't angry. I wasn't sad, either. I only felt great compassion for her. As I noticed this and wondered why I felt no anger, I realized that she was exuding so much shame that all I could feel was compassion. Much as I'd like to say that I normally react to those who've "wronged me" with pure compassion, that would be untrue. I have a part that has big antennae guarding against those who would "do me wrong." So this reaction was very curious to me.

That's when it hit me. I realized in that moment that I could remember a time in my life when I felt that kind of shame. I remembered the "Jeremy years" as it all came flooding back — all the moments of shame and humiliation, the fear, the self-loathing, the feeling that I carried of wanting it all to end and to crawl out of my own skin.

I told Kerri that I wasn't angry and that I hoped she'd be easy on herself. I hoped with all my heart that she would quickly get past all that she carried.

It's clear to me that I had judged this moment as a great opportunity to be reintroduced to that time in my life and to let my Protective Part know that it would be okay to let all of it back in now because now I could handle it. It was time. I was an adult, and I could return to the events and look at them with compassion rather than self-loathing. I could feel compassion for that eight-year-old boy and the feeling I'd carried with me all those years of being ashamed, alone, and believing I had nowhere to turn. There was nothing to forgive. Now I could thank my Protective Part, grieve for the suffering of that period of my life, and celebrate the relief and unburdening from that pain.

A final note: For the purposes of this story, I felt that it was important to be honest about my own thoughts, feelings, and actions, and to confront the truth of my own context and that of my contemporaries: that homophobia was tragically, unapologetically prevalent in those times. I join in the celebration that times have dramatically changed and that children are decreasingly confronted with such hatred and bigotry toward gay and lesbian people.

We all have parts that work to make the best out of the traumatic events that come our way. This story of parts protecting a young boy is ultimately an example of how we can love and trust our own parts to do what's needed and to take control and make the best of a terrible, hurtful series of experiences.

Our parts not only allow us to survive in the face of difficult odds, but they also navigate the best way to survive, given the trauma we've encountered, even if it leads to repressing the events themselves and not feeling the pain at all. While this doesn't come without a price — in Michael's case, a harsh change in his thoughts, feelings, and actions during his adolescence — it does allow us time to cope with the pain and suffering.

Chapter 7

Parts and Compassion

Embracing the "parts approach" frequently gives people a different way to relate not only to themselves and their spouses but to others as well. In particular, it becomes easier to be more compassionate as one begins to recognize some of one's own parts in others. Here's the story of a T-ball coach who experiences this firsthand.

I was coaching T-ball one spring with a new group of boys when one of the fathers approached me to introduce himself. Doug was very outgoing and supportive, and he seemed to want to be involved with the team. His son, Doug Junior, was shy and somewhat smaller than many of the other boys.

After a couple of practices, it became apparent that Doug Senior was not happy with his son's athletic abilities, and he began to coach him from the sidelines, often yelling instructions on how to make a better swing at the ball or how to hold his glove to catch a grounder. This reached a crescendo during our first game when Doug Junior dropped a pop-up fly ball. His father, furious, threw his cap to the ground and stalked away from the first base sideline, where he had been on patrol. At the end of the inning, Doug Junior was visibly upset and withdrew. He told me he didn't want to play anymore. Luckily, I needed to substitute another boy in anyway, so that was the end of it — for the time being.

After the game, I spoke with Doug Senior and gently suggested that he might want to give his son a little more time to hone his skills. He nodded in agreement and looked away at Doug Junior walking back toward their car.

At the next practice, Doug Senior was back on the first base sideline, shouting instructions to his son. I found myself getting more and more irritated. I saw one of the other fathers walk up to Doug and speak with him. Both men seemed uncomfortable, and the conversation ended with the other father walking away as Doug resumed his stream of helpful hints. Now I was truly angry. At the end of practice, I walked up to Doug and let him have it, asking him if he knew what a jerk he was, whether he knew what damage he was doing to his son's self-confidence, and how he was singlehandedly ruining things for everyone. Predictably, Doug returned fire, telling me that I was a pussy and a shitty coach, and that all the boys needed to learn how to take some real coaching, like the kind they'll get when they're older.

Driving home, I began to think about what had happened. Why did I let my temper take over? Why, as the coach, didn't I model for the team how to handle a difference of opinion? I felt I had made a bad mistake. Why?

Later that evening, as I was making dinner, the answer just somehow occurred to me. I wasn't even thinking about the incident — it just popped into my consciousness like a mental tap on the shoulder. "Hey, pal, you were an athlete in high school and college, and you were ultracompetitive. You have two sons, and you're ultracompetitive for them, even though you don't let anyone see that part of you. You aren't proud of that part. It also brings along memories of being humiliated by mistakes during various games, of looking over at your own father on the sideline after a missed tackle. So, how different is this part of you from Doug?"

This was an unsettling insight. But in a way that's hard to describe, it gave me some kind of emotional insight. Perhaps the way to relate to Doug Senior was to have more empathy for the part of him that is out of control and to try to help him, as best I could, become aware of its effect on his son.

The T-ball coach experienced a common shift in awareness that comes with the "parts approach." Once you begin to get to know your own parts, it's easier to see and have appreciation and compassion for others' parts. This is especially true for behavior in others that you may find objectionable. If you take the time to fully relate to these people through the lens of parts, your struggles with your own problematic behaviors can provide a touchstone for understanding and better communication.

The next time you're angered or annoyed by someone else's extreme behavior, try to remember that it doesn't mean they're jerks. Most likely, it means they have parts in distress.

Chapter 8

Parts and the Workplace

Our relationships with others at our place of work bring special challenges that often require a delicate mix of interpersonal skills. Whether you're working for someone or managing direct reports or both, the "parts approach" can be extremely valuable.

Peter is a seasoned manager who has learned how to turn many people's tendency to explain difficult work situations in terms of parts into "teachable moments."

I've been a manager in different organizations for over thirty years. Most anyone with my experience will tell you that the hardest part of managing a team, a department, or an entire company is managing people. Over the years, I've attended many seminars, been mentored by my managers, and read many books, but for me the single most intuitively understandable and most effective approach to dealing with people issues in a business setting is the concept of parts. I believe this is true because so many people are already familiar with the concept—even if they're not aware of it!

Not long ago, a direct supervisee of mine, Mary, came into my office and sat down. Mary and I had worked together for several years and had developed a very friendly and trusting relationship. She looked at me nervously and said, "I have to go talk to George about the decision I've made to terminate his research. Part of me wants to go and talk to him right now and get this over with, and another part of me wants nothing at all to do with talking to him and thinks I should maybe just send him an email. I'm not sure how to handle this."

I could see that Mary was very nervous and didn't have her usual decisiveness.

"Tell me about the parts you just mentioned," I said.

"Well, one part doesn't want to talk to George—doesn't like conflict, especially with George. He's one of the original members of this group and feels entitled. He can be very difficult to deal with; he's a yeller sometimes. The part that wants to talk to him now thinks that I don't have the courage to do it."

I asked Mary which part seemed to have the upper hand, and she said definitely the "Don't Talk to George" Part. I asked her why. "I don't like confrontation. I mean, you know, who does? It's always been hard for me, I guess, for as long as I can remember." She told me that she frequently delayed confrontation, which usually made things worse.

I then asked if she could tell me more about the Critical Part and what she thought it needed. She thought for a moment: "What it needs — I'm not sure what you mean. I guess it thinks I shouldn't be afraid and doesn't like the other part always caving in. It wants a say in the situation."

"That makes sense to me. Does it to you?"

Mary answered yes.

We sat there for a moment. Mary's expression softened, and she sat back in her chair. I asked her how she felt about having to talk to George now.

Mary said, "I guess I'm kind of relieved somehow. I get the both-sides thing with this. Thanks, Boss."

Later that day, Mary did talk to George. No argument, no yelling, and although it was uncomfortable for Mary, the conversation went well enough. A week or so later, George and I were seated next to each other at a company lunch. During the meal, out of nowhere George said: "You know, I'm not working on my original research project anymore. But as Mary pointed out to me, the company's priorities have changed, not that I exactly agree with that. But good kid, Mary. Handles herself well."

Peter's experience with Mary suggests that the most effective way to lead people is to help them understand their own parts — in effect, to help those we lead to lead themselves. By asking Mary about her self-described parts, Peter gently steered her toward a better understanding of her own internal world, which was essential to her ability to decide whether or not to approach George and, once she decided to approach him, how to present her decision.

Intellectually, Mary knew that she'd never done well with conflict. But when she was able to hear herself say out loud that she didn't like conflict and that George could be scary, and also hear herself speak for another part of her that wanted a "say" in the situation and didn't like to cave in, she had a moment of realization.

As Peter validated that this made sense to both of them, Mary relaxed and gained strength from recognizing what her parts were feeling, even though they were opposed to one another (in other words, that one wanted to avoid conflict, while the other wanted to deal with it and have the confidence and calm to do so).

This process of speaking for our parts and saying out loud with clarity what our parts want, what they want to do, and how they differ from one another, is immensely helpful in preparing for difficult decisions. It's highly likely that we'd see a much different outcome if Mary had followed her conflict-avoidant impulse not to deal with George directly. She would have felt that she'd failed as a manager and failed to move the project in the direction she knew was right for the company. However, we also can see that if she'd launched into the conflict with George without acknowledging this conflict avoidance, it's very likely that she wouldn't have been able to "handle herself well," and her discussion with George wouldn't have made her decision clear and final.

> *The process of speaking for our parts and saying out loud what our parts want is immensely helpful in preparing for difficult decisions.*

It can be easy to misinterpret people's motives in a workplace setting. A top priority for one party may be a minor detail to another. A "parts approach" to staying focused on the desired outcome rather than emotional reactions to perceived slights can go a long way, as Sean's story illustrates.

It had been almost a year, and two invoices from my refrigeration maintenance company had not been paid. Sure, some invoices take a while to be paid, and that's to be expected — but a year?

We'd presented photos, documentation, signed work orders, invoices — everything normally required. In return, we received inane emails that didn't address key questions, as if their strategy was to wear us out so we would just give up and forget the whole thing! As more emails weren't responded to, I attempted to draw more people into the loop in search of payment. Then one day I received an email from their head person saying that he was the only person I was allowed to communicate with about these bills — no one else.

I was furious. First they jerk us around, then give us the silent treatment, and finally only one point of contact. This is not how anyone treats a courteous, reliable business relationship. Then I found myself thinking what a wonderful feeling it was to be furious — lots of energy, lots of focus. I thought to myself, "They're going to pay, no matter what, and I'll make certain that this happens." It feels so good, so right, to be self-righteously angry.

I composed an email from this angry, self-assured place within me and sent it to my bookkeeper for review and feedback before sending it to the company. She wrote back, "Sounds aggressive, Sean."

Then I noticed a little, quiet part of me that said, "Slow down. What are you really trying to accomplish? Do you want to destroy your entire relationship with these people?" My angry part didn't care — it wanted to fight for fairness and justice. Yes, fairness and justice are wanted, and no, compromise does not feel appropriate. I did more quiet noticing within, and the little, quiet part of me continued to speak, for a change! It said that respect is also wanted, and it questioned whether I was being respectful. Who is this little voice within? What is this all about?

Okay, this thing is bigger and different than I had imagined. Some parts of me are very uncomfortable with the Angry Part getting its way, even though they appreciate its energy and focus. These same parts of me wanted to write the email. The email read: "Part of me is surprised and sad that we are still having this discussion, and another part of me knows you are doing your best. Respectfully, Sean." Two hours later, I received an email saying that both invoices are being resent to the initiating department for review and resolution. My bookkeeper's response: "That's the email we've been watching for."

I yielded, which isn't compromising, criticizing, or blaming. It's noticing and speaking for parts of me — especially parts that I have ignored for most of my life, particularly under stress.

As children, most of us are taught to learn the difference between right and wrong. We learn to follow rules and to behave in pro-social ways—ways that serve the greatest good for ourselves and all those with whom we interact. We learn that there's a right way to do things and a wrong way, and we learn to be fair, to share, and to take turns. We get very good at detecting when others don't conform to these teachings, especially when we're the victims of their behavior. When that happens, we can get angry and self-righteous.

Those of us who are taught this way as children typically have childlike parts that become activated in the face of others treating us unfairly, and those parts get incensed when they realize they're being treated that way, especially when under stress. These parts want justice and respect. They will not be taken advantage of! Just think of a road rager flipping the bird at another driver for cutting in front of him "unfairly" or a dissatisfied customer yelling at a service person over a perceived product defect.

Whether behind the wheel of our car or in the customer service line, the vast majority of us are old enough and evolved enough to have the capacity for empathy, patience, and compassion. We understand that the world is rarely black and white. So how do we find ourselves led by a childlike part that is out for justice at the expense of our better judgment? How do we manage to become a raving lunatic in the car, only to park the car in the parking lot, walk into a building, and literally within three minutes become this other shy, polite, reserved person on the elevator? It's because these childlike parts who know what's right and wrong and who demand justice are such an important part of our upbringing and so entrenched in us that they have a way of popping up with great passion and certainty to protect us from being "taken advantage of" or "victimized." They seek easy examples of right and wrong where nuance isn't necessary, and they pounce.

Sean's Justice Part was triggered and was poised to pounce on the powers that be at the contracting company. Sean's money was being withheld, and they were wrong! Sean prepared to attack from his Justice Part. He would have been "right" to do so. But would he have been smart? Would he achieve the outcome he wanted?

When Sean was nudged by his bookkeeper—"Sounds aggressive," she'd said—Sean paused. Rather than ask, "Who's right?" Sean asked, "What's the outcome I'm looking for?" Sean abandoned the "wonderful feeling" of being right (and yes, what a wonderful feeling it is when we know we're right!) and focused on how best to recoup the money owed him, which was his primary objective.

Sean's perfectly worded email—"Part of me is surprised and sad that we are still having this discussion, and another part of me knows you are doing your best. Respectfully, Sean"—acknowledged both of his parts: the part that knows he's right and the part that expresses compassion and genuine regard for the recipient. Sean was able to speak for his parts and to do so from a position of respect and understanding. In so doing, he elevated the communication to a higher level of understanding. Sean was able to top the old adage "It's better to be smart than right" by being both smart and right.

> *Rather than ask, "Who's right?" Sean asked, "What's the outcome I'm looking for?"*

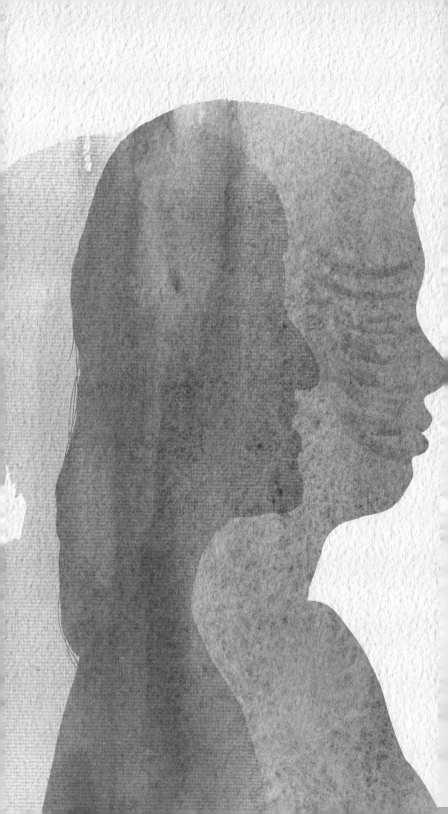

CHAPTER 9

Parts and Illness

FACING ILLNESS, ESPECIALLY SERIOUS or life-threatening illness, is a life-changing event. It has a way of stripping away our defenses and denial of vulnerability in a flash and exposing our fears and insecurities in ways we have not experienced before. People manage these episodes in different ways, some gracious and others not. But when faced with bad news that cuts to the core, understanding how one's parts react can be insightful, hopeful, and liberating.

Many people face the daunting task of dealing with cancer. Especially challenging are tests that present ambiguous results when the worst may be possible but not certain. Cancer, as with many issues with our physical health, makes understanding and appreciating one's internal parts invaluable.

Maxine, a 52-year-old mother of two, tells the following:

> Five years ago, doctors found a cancerous tumor on my thymus gland. It was removed with a horrendous surgery that involved sawing my chest open and "chicken wiring" it back together. The doctors said that this cancer tends to come back but isn't noticeable for many years, as it is so slow growing.

Last summer, after packing up both my daughters to leave for college for the first time, I went in for my annual CT scan and follow-up appointment with my surgeon. He said, "Everything looks good at a quick glance. We just have to wait for the radiology report, but maybe we can go two years until your next scan." I was shocked when, a few days later, his office called and said, "The doctor wants you to come in for a PET scan. It looks like there has been a recurrence."

Of course, my head went reeling, "My cancer can't be back!" My husband's stance was, "Let's not jump to conclusions. We can take care of whatever comes." My Protective Part didn't want to tell my daughters for fear they would refuse to head off for college and want to stay home with me. I knew I couldn't tell my mother about the latest scan because she was just leaving for a two-week trip, and I knew if I told her about my vague test results, she would spend her whole holiday worrying.

Two weeks later, kids safely at college, the results from the PET scan were in, and this time my husband came with me to the doctor's office to hear the results. "We can't be certain the cancer is back," my surgeon stated. "There appears to be some growth since last year's scan, but it could just be a shift in the scar tissue, or it could be a bad scan. It's not a place we can biopsy, and since it's a slow-growing cancer, the best thing to do is to just wait a year and scan again." Wait a year? I had just spent two anxiety-filled weeks waiting for the PET scan results, and now he wanted me to stretch it out for another year, not knowing whether the cancer was back or not?

After this news, I felt as though I was walking around in an emotional haze. I didn't tell many people because what do you say? "I may have cancer . . . I won't know for a year . . . I may need sympathy and support, I may not." Internally, I could feel my parts at war with each other:

"The cancer is back . . . this is the beginning of the end!"

"Don't be silly. You heard the doctor—it could just be a shift in scar tissue."

After a couple of weeks of fretting, obsessing, debating, and sleepless nights, I wasn't sure how I would survive this for a year. Finally, I decided to stop the cycle and just listen to the part of me that was convinced I had cancer.

"What makes you think I have cancer?" I asked.

"I don't think I have cancer, I KNOW I have cancer, and the rest of you won't listen to me!"

"Well, I'm listening now. I get it—you're certain I have cancer. You KNOW it for sure. Well, if that's the case, we can do cancer. We've done it before. We'll change the agenda and go into cancer-fighting mode."

Suddenly the part felt heard, and I could feel it relax. The amazing thing was, all of the stress, tension, and obsession began to disappear after that. I was able to sleep again. Once I accepted the part that said I have cancer, that anxious part calmed down, felt heard and responded to, and no longer felt as if it needed to be in the lead.

I still don't know if I have cancer. I'm waiting for my next scan later this summer, but I can acknowledge all of my parts: "Anxious, I Have Cancer," "Optimistic, Don't Think the Worst Unless Proven to Be True," "Worrier and Protector," and the managerial "We Can Take Care of This" one as well. Being able to separate from my parts enough to listen to them without being emotionally hijacked by them has enabled me to live my life despite facing an uncertain future.

In this story, Maxine is confronted with a dreadful mixture of circumstances. The life-and-death magnitude of the issue—cancer—combined with the one-year wait could paralyze the best of us with anxiety for what may come. Add to this the curious place that she finds herself in with regard to others. She finds it hard to solicit support from outside because people might struggle to feel profound compassion for someone who "might have cancer."

Not surprisingly, Maxine hears from many of her parts in the face of this situation. They're loud, and they're in conflict. We see the "cycle" of parts similar to what we've seen in previous stories: we see the Anxiety ("I have cancer"), the Hope ("Don't think the worst unless proven to be true"), and the Plan ("We can take care of this"). This isn't surprising because it's natural for parts to become triggered in the face of threats to our well-being.

If we really bring our best empathy to this situation, we can see how hard this must have been for Maxine and why it's common for people to respond poorly to situations when our parts get the best of us. The Anxiety continues to eat away at us ("We definitely have cancer") while the Hope fights back ("You don't know that—maybe we don't have cancer"), and we let our parts battle it out until the day the test results come back. While it's easy to see how this can and often does happen, it certainly is a recipe for a very bad year for Maxine, were she to succumb to this spiral of her parts at war.

But instead, Maxine does a very wise thing: She stops and listens to all of her parts and pays particular attention to the Anxiety Part that is most triggered by her circumstance. We can almost sense Maxine asking her other parts to hold back so that she can really hear her Anxiety Part clearly. When she asks her Anxiety Part, it reports to her, "I don't think I have cancer, I KNOW I have cancer!" We can also almost feel Maxine's other parts, including her Hope Part, wanting to shout down her Anxiety Part ("Stop being so doom and gloom"), but Maxine doesn't allow this bickering to continue. Instead, she bears witness to her Anxiety Part, and while assuring it that she's listening, tells it, "We can do cancer. We've done it before."

With Maxine's recounting of this moment, we can palpably feel her Anxiety Part relax, knowing that it was heard, was taken seriously, and was ultimately responsible for the course that Maxine would set: to go into cancer-fighting mode.

By listening to her parts and making a decision based on what they all had to say, Maxine came to a well-considered decision about how she'd act in the year to come while waiting to find out if she had a recurrence of cancer. She is very clear that without this respect for and curiosity about her parts, it would have been much more difficult for her to set a course to "live my life despite facing an uncertain future."

While we can't control all that life brings us, we can empower ourselves to face the unknown and the anxiety that comes with the unknown by allowing our parts to be heard and respected. They want what's best for us, even when they seem at odds. If they feel heard and witnessed, they'll not only allow us to more peacefully follow a course of action that we choose, they'll relax and become part of the process rather than compound the problem.

> *We can empower ourselves to face the unknown by allowing our parts to be heard and respected.*

Chapter 10

Parts and Parenting

For those of you who have raised children, you are already aware of the many emotions that come into play between parent and child. At once your most beloved beings, they can get under your skin as no others can. Frequently, a parent's relationship to his or her own parents becomes a "part" in the family dynamic. This was the case with Jocelyn.

I learned about my parts as a result of the birth of my children, now five and nine years old. Prior to having kids, I had had my share of failed intimate relationships. I entered therapy and "worked out my issues," or so I thought. I eventually was able to find a loving, kind person with whom I fit well, and for several years thereafter we built a life together that was quite good and for the most part conflict-free. We got married and decided to start a family.

Things started getting really difficult for me after our first son was about two years of age. As I look back on it now, it was all part of normal childhood development. However, at the time, I didn't have that perspective. I wasn't used to people in my life yelling at me or hitting me when they were upset or when I told them no. I also wasn't used to piercing high-pitched screams when someone got overly excited about something. I was getting triggered. My child was activating things in me that I didn't even know existed.

I'd heard several people say that parenting is the best of times and the worst of times. Well, I was certainly experiencing both. At times I was acting in ways that were shocking to me, yelling and having tantrums of my own! I found that I was asking myself: Who have I become? What is happening to me? I didn't like the way I was responding to my child, whom I loved more than life itself.

Our second son, who was born four years later with special needs, was challenging for me on a whole different level. He forced me to dig deeper and, with the help of IFS, to explore the young, wounded parts of me that were hit, treated badly, and yelled at as a child. I learned that I had repressed most of those early memories. I learned that my kids were activating my wounded parts and that my Protective Parts were trying to keep me safe by trying to stop my present-day offenders (my children) from recreating my own childhood. As a result of this awareness, our family started using "parts" language. What a relief to know that it wasn't all of me, or all of my spouse, or even all of my children—it was "a part of us" at any particular moment expressing one aspect of what we were feeling.

Our kids took to the "parts" language quite easily; it almost seemed natural to them as we introduced it into our regular family dialogue. My kids learned that when we were upset with one another, it was "a part" of us that was engaging with the other, not "all of us," and the same was true for them.

I'll never forget what my younger son said to me after one of my not-so-great parenting moments, when I yelled at him for taking his brother's Lego and throwing it down the stairs. He said, "Hey, Momma, you still love me even when I don't behave all the time, right?" I stopped in my tracks, instantly melting and saying to him, "Yes, honey, you're absolutely right. A part of Momma got mad at you for throwing your brother's toy, but of course I still love you and always will." "That's what I thought," he said as we hugged each other with big smiles on our faces. He readily returned the Lego and apologized to his brother. It was in that moment that I said to myself: "I will not repeat my history with my children."

One generally accepted notion for how we raise our children is that we can cause great shame and pain if we're overly critical of them. Instead, when we tell children that we don't like what they did, but we still love them, we help children understand that it's possible to do a bad thing and still be a good person. Among the many redeeming aspects of viewing ourselves and others through the lens of parts is that it is easy for children to grasp this idea. Jocelyn's son can see that, while angering his mom, he's not a bad person, and his mom loves him.

By embracing the "parts approach," and by having an understanding of her own parts, Jocelyn brings a foundation of understanding and self-acceptance into her role as a parent. What pains and burdens do we carry as a result of harmful messages from our parents? What parts do we have that protect us from these harmful experiences?

There may be no greater preparation for parenting than to understand our own parts, especially those that were influenced, or even scarred, as children. If we understand how we behaved as children and how we were parented in response to our childhood behavior, we can sort out what worked and what didn't. Jocelyn brings this awareness to the table in her parenting. She uncovers the pain of her own childhood and, by using parts language with her son, is able to avoid the pitfalls of relating to her children in ways that caused her pain as a child.

> *There may be no greater preparation for parenting than to understand our own parts.*

Conclusion

WE LIVE IN A WORLD IN WHICH WE'RE CONSTANTLY encouraged to view ourselves and others as being primarily one aspect of our personality. "That guy is just a drunk!" "It's a good thing she's such a good athlete, 'cause otherwise she'd be a zero." "At least I can play guitar." This way of thinking is very convenient and takes little work, but it's a negative and harmful way to view ourselves and each another.

The notion that we all have parts and that these subpersonalities dwell within all of us can be difficult to accept. Yet we hear the internal dialogue of our thoughts virtually every waking moment, and we know that our internal voices speak to us in many different ways—different ideas, advice, emotions, and varying degrees of intensity, given the circumstances. We hear from our parts all the time, and we often feel our parts in our bodies as well.

Once we accept our parts, we can begin to learn about them. Like all relationships, we can help our parts that experience extreme emotions or burdens by listening to them and attending to them, as we would any person we care about. When our parts lead us astray, we can assist them in understanding why their desires are misguided while at the same time keeping in mind that our parts always want what's best for us. We can then help our parts shift, which in turn is how we ourselves can change.

Have you ever had someone confide in you, revealing a negative part of their personality, perhaps admitting they were an alcoholic, a workaholic, or an overeater? Next time this happens, try telling the person that you don't see them that way—rather, you see them as a person who has a part that pushes them to drink, or work, or eat. Watch and see if the person doesn't show a palpable sense of relief and gratitude for you for seeing them this way. We all have an internal dread of being labeled as one thing, but no one is a single trait, behavior, or opinion. When we know we aren't just one thing, we are liberated from the bounds of that label, and we see ourselves and others with greater compassion.

Learning about our own parts, listening to them, and learning that others have parts allows us to find genuine compassion and calm within. It creates a foundation of strength and serenity upon which we can rely for our entire lives, and it also enables us to extend love, compassion, calm, strength, and serenity to others.

About IFS

IFS (INTERNAL FAMILY SYSTEMS) is a psychotherapeutic modality developed by Dr. Richard Schwartz in the mid-1980s. Over the past thirty years, IFS has evolved into a comprehensive approach that includes clear methods and guidelines for working with individuals, couples, and families. It is now practiced by thousands of therapists worldwide. Close to 50 professional trainers currently teach the IFS Model across the United States and in Europe and Latin America, with over 3,000 individuals having been trained to date. For more information about IFS, please visit the Center for Self Leadership website, www.selfleadership.org.

THE FOUNDATION FOR SELF LEADERSHIP, an independent 501(c)(3) nonprofit organization registered in the State of Illinois in 1999, is dedicated to advancing IFS by supporting research and scholarship outreach. For more information, please visit the Foundation for Self Leadership website, www.foundationifs.org.

About the Authors

JON SCHWARTZ, MED, has worked in the mental health field for over 30 years, both as a clinician and in leadership positions within mental health organizations. Jon began his directorship of the Center for Self Leadership in 2008. Jon lives in Salem, Oregon.

BILL BRENNAN, MFA, has over 30 years of experience in media and content/product development, including executive positions at Health Dialog, Harvard Business School, WGBH Boston, and the ABC and NBC Television Networks. His broadcast programs, websites, and interactive media tools have won over 100 national and international awards.